Mother's NEST

PROPHETESS MABEL ZANGO TANYE-KULONO

PROPHETESS
MABEL ZANGO TANYE-KULONO

Mother's Nest
The uniqueness of a woman A woman, but a builder
characteristic of a good woman Her modest outward
appearance setting proper priories prayer line
by Mabel Zango Tanye-kulomo

Printed in the United States of America.

ISBN 9781498481045

Unless otherwise indicated, Scripture quotations taken from
Scripture quotations taken from the New King James Version
(NKJV). Copyright © 1982 by Thomas Nelson, Inc. Used by
permission. All rights reserved.

Author's Information: Web: www.covenantdestiny.com
Email:covenantdestiny39@yahoo.com
Prayer line: + 857-216-2464 Pin: 31297

Developed and Designed by Repu-Build Africa Ltd.
Website: repubuildafricagh.com
Email: info@repubuildafricagh.com
Tel: +233 303 - 966 436 / +233 269-212 518 / +233 554-643 954

REFERENCE:
This book was greatly inspired by Vickie Kraft's (2009) write up on
"making a house a home"-The Influential Woman: Thomas Nelson.
http://bible.org/seriespage/lesson-7-making-house-home.

CONTENT

"Mothers Nest" is dedicated to women all over the world seeking to get it right in their marriages. It is also dedicated to all the young ladies who want to grow to be women that influence the world positively in God. I again dedicate this book to all the men and women of God I have known all my life and who have in diverse ways taught and guided me.

Finally, I dedicate this book to my husband, Col. Paul Tanye-Kulono and my children (Barbara, Paulette, Marvin and Mikayla). I love you all.

━━━━ ACKNOWLEDGEMENT ━━━━

I would like to first and foremost thank the almighty God for the wisdom and knowledge He granted me to put this book together.

I sincerely want to acknowledge Mr Chris Wilmont, Reverend Father David Bagsiibu, Bishop Gideon Thomas Gyamfi, General and Mrs Saagbul, Pastor Stephen Aryitey, Prophet Aaron, Apostle Joshua Cobbinah Christensen, Kwabena Oteng, Pastor Sammy, Pastor Innocent Fasemkye, Rev. Godfred Mensah, Mrs Sussie Adisah Mahama, Pastor Wisdom Anane, Grace Brown Smith, Elizabeth Ngugi and all members of Covenant Destiny Ministries (CDM) for their immense inspiration and support.

Finally, I want to acknowledge my mother, my brothers and sisters for being there for me. I am very grateful to you all.

—— **FOREWORD BY** ——

Dr. Joyce R. Aryee
[OVC, FIPR, FGIM, Fcia, FGHIE]
Management and Communications Consultant
and
C.E.O – Salt and Light Ministries International

FOREWORD

Many things are said about women and much of the said things are not very positive because of negative stereotypes. Some believe that women are one of God's most complicated creations and others hold on to a belief that women are powerful but, use their power for destruction. Not "Mothers Nest". In this book, the author makes us see the best side of women–people who are indeed God's special creation.

Prophetess Tanye-Kulono, a married woman and a mother gives us a portrayal of womanhood from a simple but, very biblical perspective. She teaches women how to carry themselves and add value and worth to their lives. Alas, many women miss the point of how valuable they are to God and humanity and therefore, allow themselves to be taken for granted. This book emphasizes that, women have been created for a purpose. Women have been created to stand up and be counted as people who have been gifted to contribute to the development of nations in our generation. The author encourages us to step into the light of God and understand our purpose.

Prophetess Mabel Zango Tanye-Kulono's "Mother's Nest" is a must read for not only women, but, also for men who want to relate with women for the purpose of a better understanding of a woman's psyche. This is an amazing book because, it guides us through the journey of life and makes women creatures of love, power, compassion and therefore, worthy to play useful roles in our society.

─────── INTRODUCTION ───────

"Mother's Nest" is a must read Christian book that draws inspiration from the Holy Bible and seeks to help readers have a clear and biblical understanding about why God created a woman (Genesis 2:18). The book further seeks to present a Biblical perspective of the reason why a woman was created in that unique way of being formed from the rib bone of a man.

Every woman is a potential mother and has the possibility of exhibiting skills of motherhood. A mother is a woman who has raised a child, whether her own biological child or not. This implies that any woman who helps in the raising up of any child and practically takes part in the upbringing of responsible children, in my opinion, is a mother. As a mother, one of your crucial responsibilities is to ensure that your dependants are safe and properly housed. It is the reason why this book also aligns itself with how birds in the air house their offspring.

Birds in their world, in an attempt to provide a safe place for their breed, weave nests.

The nest is a form of shelter used by these birds for the purpose of raising their offspring. When birds breed by producing eggs, the eggs need to be kept warm until they are hatched.

Therefore, it becomes the responsibility of one or both parents to sit on the eggs for a set period of time, allowing the embryos to develop into chicks (baby birds). It is not possible to balance an egg on a perch. So the nest is built to hold the eggs during the incubation period and to protect the young birds until they are old enough to fly. This scenario is clearly accounted for in the Holy Bible (Matthew *8:20*). Similarly, this book takes a critical look at the 'Proverbs 31' woman in the Bible and how we all must endeavour to emulate her enviable virtues.

This book also seeks to inspire all women, married or not, to take charge of their homes and build an environment that promotes Godly relationships. It further argues that, the entire family's life must be one that God is pleased with. Reading through the various chapters, it is made clear that, several situations will come up to frustrate you, or several attempts can be made to keep you away from your

marital home, children and spouse. All these notwithstanding, you must bear in mind that you need to build a home for your family. You cannot fail them, hence, no matter the situation, you must strive to overcome it to keep your family intact.

The author outlines how God has always favoured women. She [the author] also presents an assurance of how God will help every woman achieve more in life like the "Proverbs 31" woman, if his presence is sought in all decisions. Again, the author through this book, is admonishing all women to be up and doing and must strive to achieve more in addition to raising children. Considering the author's own experience and deep interaction with many women, she is clear in her mind that raising children is a career. She however, explains practically, how idle a woman can become in a matter of time, if other careers are not developed in addition to raising children.

Under the heading *Prayer Lines,* this book leads the reader through series of prayers the author believes will save and turn situations round if faith is exercised. These are prayers that when said in challenging times moves God to prove himself strong.

As Christians, we need to draw reasonable lessons from other people's experiences to shape our lives. With illustrations from practical and true life situations, the author presents how prayer and endurance leads to overcoming evil plots against marriages; it also presents principles for building a successful family. Simple but deep and sincere explanations are presented about how the favour gained from God during creation qualifies all women who are determined to achieve their aims and aspirations, can outweigh the achievements of the woman in Proverbs 31.

As you read this book, I hope and pray that you will be clear in your mind about the mystery of womanhood and how women are favoured.

1

THE
UNIQUENESS
OF A WOMAN

CHAPTER ONE

THE UNIQUENESS OF A WOMAN

Genesis 2:18
"And the Lord God said, "It is not good that man should be alone; I will make him a helper comparable to him."

The Bible in Genesis 2:18, states categorically that, a woman was created as a companion and helper to man. Based on accounts in the Bible, it is worth noting that the creation of woman was unique and symbolic.

The first woman was made from Adam's ribs, and not from his head to rule over him. Not from his feet to be trampled upon, but from his side, to walk side by side with him as a true companion and a helper. I have no doubt that, it is for this singular reason that the Bible says:

"*He who finds a wife finds a good thing and receives favour from the lord. Proverbs 18:22*".

God has already in his word liberated women because, there cannot be any greater responsibility than carrying a baby for several months and after delivery, nurturing and moulding that soul in a way that will glorify God. Due to God's favour on women, God considered women worthy in His plan of bringing redemption to mankind (Genesis 3:15) and when the fullness of time came, God sent forth His only begotten son born of a woman to bring salvation to the world (Galatians 4:4).

God entrusted the conception and the caring of the Saviour in the hands of a woman. It is therefore not out of place that a woman at one time is known as a daughter, a sister, wife, a mother, a companion and a helper. I must also say that, women possess qualities that naturally make them powerful and influential. As women, we have the ability to influence and turn situations around in the world. It is therefore not surprising at all that, God used us (women) in saving the world from condemnation. God has a way of dealing with every situation. And in His wisdom could have given the Saviour to the world by showing Him on a door of a faithful or a great prophet, like he gave a ram to Abraham to be sacrificed in place of Isaac.

"Abraham looked up and there in a thicket he saw a ram caught by his horns. He went over and took the ram and sacrificed it as a burnt offering instead of his son" (Genesis 22:13).

God could have also provided or better still "rained" the Saviour on us in the same way as he did manna for the people of Israel in the wilderness.

"Then the Lord said to Moses. "Behold, I will rain bread from heaven for you. And the people shall go out and gather a certain quota every day, that I may test them, whether they will walk in my law or not"

(Exodus 16:4).In a different account, God commanded ravens to feed Elijah when he was running away from Jezebel.

"And the word of the LORD came unto him, saying, get thee hence, and turn thee eastward, and hide thyself by the brook Cherith that is before Jordan. And it shall be, that thou shalt drink of the brook; and I have commanded the ravens to feed thee there. So he went and did according unto the word of the LORD: For he went and dwelt by the brook Cherith that is before Jordan" (1 kings 17: 2-5).

From the Biblical examples above, and in several instances, God has proven that He is God by doing wonders in providing miraculous solutions to situations. But, God had a special purpose for women for which reason he created Eve the way He did. It took a woman to bring forth the Saviour of the world, Jesus Christ. Mary was highly favoured, thus, God gave her a special honour to bear Jesus, our Messiah. In the same light, God has given all women this special honour that Mary had to beget the saviour.

And having come in, the angel said to her, "Rejoice, highly favoured one, the Lord is with you; blessed are you among women!" But, when she saw him, she was troubled at his saying, and considered what manner of greetings this was. Then the angel said to her, "Do not be afraid, Mary, for you have found favour with God." And behold, you will conceive in your womb and bring forth a son, and shall call His name JESUS. He will be great, and will be called the son of the Highest; and the Lord God will give Him the throne of His father David" (Luke 1:28-32).

The Bible, in Proverbs 31 talks about the virtuous woman, a woman with great strength. As Christians, we should all take a look at how the Bible described the qualities of the virtuous woman and emulate her. A Godly woman as described by the Bible, is devoted to God, her husband, children and family. As a Godly woman you are required to ensure that your family is secured and well protected. To achieve this, the virtuous woman creates a *"nest"* for the family to be able to live peacefully and happily and to go on with their religious duties.

Women, I urge you to remain faithful to God and your husbands. Be honest, be gentle, and stay away from unnecessary gossip and unnecessary association with friends. Be confident and don't ever feel intimidated by anyone at work, in the home or anywhere you find yourself. Practice self-control, be generous, take your place in the building of the nest, promote unity and keep your family safe in the nest.

After the death of Joshua, the Israelites were oppressed, and they cried out to the Lord for deliverance. It once again took a woman, Deborah to communicate to God and gather an army to mount Tabor to fight (Judges 4:9). God in the Bible has used several women to achieve His numerous plans. However, the women used were of noble character. Humble and meek women were used by God to carry out his plan. Avail therefore yourself to be used by God as instruments for his purpose.

This requires courage and initiative. Every wise woman builds her home, but the foolish one plucks it down with her hands. Be vigilant as women and keep an eye on the petty tricks of the devil that make us sometimes feel that we are incapable, depressed and unworthy to execute anything for God. Remember that the devil is a LIAR! Women, we are more than able!

2

A
WOMAN,
BUT A BUILDER

CHAPTER TWO

A WOMAN,
BUT A BUILDER

Proverbs 14:1
*"The wise woman builds her
house, but with her own hands
the foolish one tears hers down"*

THE WISE HOUSE-BUILDER

A wise woman can build her
house in various ways. Some of the ways are as
follows:

She seeks God's will for her life.

The wise builder (woman) prays that God will
guide every decision of hers in her service to
God. This actually involves submitting to her

husband, raising up her children in the fear of God, using her talents appropriately, shopping and putting palatable food on the table and everything that matters in her life. She actually seeks God's face in all that she does.

She seeks the spiritual riches of God through diligent prayer and learning.
"Through wisdom a house is built, and by understanding it is established; by knowledge the rooms are filled with all precious and pleasant riches" *(Proverbs 24:3-4).*

We read in the Bible (Proverbs 8:10-11) that God's instruction, knowledge, understanding and wisdom are of more value than silver, gold and rubies. As a woman who yearns to build her home spiritually, she internalizes these precious spiritual riches and uses them to build her relationship with God, her family and others.

She keeps both her physical and spiritual house clean and orderly.
Using God's Spirit, a woman guards her mind, resisting evil thoughts, gossip, slander and idle

chatter. The woman who seeks to build a spiritual home does not allow her mind to be cluttered with worldly things as the scripture says:

"Do not love the world or the things in the world. If anyone loves the world, the love of the Father is not in him. For all that is in the world the lust of the flesh, the lust of the eyes and the pride of life is not of the Father but is of the world" (1 John 2:15–16).

Again in the same Bible, it is also written that:

"If then you were raised with Christ, seek those things which are above, where Christ sitting at the right hand of God. Set your mind on things above, not on things on the earth" (Colossians 3:12).

This woman I am talking about does not allow herself to be swallowed by the things in this demanding world so as to crowd out her spiritual growth. She keeps her focus on those things that will aid her in building that spiritual nest to house her family.

She seeks ways to enhance her life as well as the lives of others.

There are many helpful things a woman can do to broaden her horizon and to enhance her life. She gets the family involved in her carrier and educational advancement as well as helping other members of the family do same.

She ensures that the pursuant of her career and other educational desires do not deny the family of their social life and fulfilment. Taking vacations and other interesting trips that are affordable must not be overshadowed by mummy's studies or development. Of course, we must apply the spiritual intent to all that we do so that things can be well balanced.

Women ye are favoured.
God in his word pronounced blessings on the woman. God said to her:

"Thy seed will crush the ugly little head of Satan and that seed is Jesus Christ. It was indeed a seed of a woman" (Genesis 3:15).

Woman, great virtue is right inside you and the devil is in the know and envious of you, because as a woman, the devil does not have the kind of future you have. Satan existed long before God created man in the garden; yet God gave man dominion over the earth. This obviously made Satan jealous and he decided to rebel against God. Harbouring this idea, the devil became more scared after the creation of woman hence, decided to use woman in his ploy to get back at God. Why? Because, the devil knew that women are precious among God's creation. Though Satan succeeded in using a woman in getting back at God, God did not get angry, rather God said:

"Women thou art favoured, thy seed will crush the ugly little head of Satan "and that seed is Jesus Christ". It was indeed a seed of a woman (Genesis 3:15).

The devil with his envious nature has been distracting women from finding that greatness and all the great virtues implanted in us as women. You might have been searching for these virtues out there, but that woman cannot be found anywhere because, you are that woman possessing all those virtues we are talking about. The real you is the precious woman God has made out of a man's rib bone. You are fearfully and wonderfully made. Be positive; focus on the things of God; create a climate through words, action and good attitude and be led by the Spirit. Even Abraham, the father of all nations, for the promise of God to be fulfilled in his life, it took a woman, his wife Sarah for God's promise about Abraham to come to pass. How was Abraham going to multiply without Sarah?

A Biblical woman's total way of life is described in Proverbs 31. The Christian woman under consideration in this book did not do everything in a day, in a month or in one year. The Bible clearly presents her character, her substance and her way of life. That is what I seek to reiterate so that, all of us as Christian women would learn from it. Indeed, these qualities are worth emulating and I just want to add that, times and seasons change, so do our achievements as individuals. What is important is our ability to accomplish what needs to be done!

There are vast scopes of interests and activities available to women which we must appreciate. I must say that these virtues existed and where available to women many years ago, therefore in contemporary times we have no excuse. God has instilled in each and every one of us different capabilities and gifts. I believe God wants us to use these abilities and interests that He has given us, as individuals to accomplish our unique duties without compulsion. We need to know that our God has much joy when we are able to do and achieve all we desire with the given capabilities provided to us by Him.

She Sails through to build her "nest".
Misunderstandings are bound to happen in any relationship, but what matters is one's ability to resolve the issue so that the relationship is not left cracked or broken. Misunderstandings can occur between you and your fiancé, you and your relatives, you and your in-laws, among you and your colleagues and sometimes among couples about child discipline. Offences are inevitable, but as Christians, we need to work hard to prevent these offences or resolve these misunderstandings as soon as possible

to prevent the situation from tripping off. In a marital home, issues such as: having a house help, having a joint bank account, what kind of food is to be prepared on a daily basis, the number of children to be raised, among others are critical issues that can easily raise unquenchable marital flames. These, when care is not taken, can lead to separation or divorce.

In my home for example, my husband and I had similar issues which could have caused us to separate or divorce, but we both realized early enough that God had a purpose for our marriage, and I personally was much interested in building a "nest" for my family. Thus, I was not ready to allow the devil to win. Remember that the devil is always ready to spill out confusion among couples, because he is the author of confusion; he is a liar and the father of liars.

"Ye are of your father the devil, and the lust of your father ye will do. He was a murderer from the beginning, and abode not in truth, because there is no truth in him. When he speaketh a lie, he speaketh of his own: for he is a liar and the father of it" (John 8:44).

Couples, let's all be careful of the words we speak to our spouses in our anger because these words have the potential of causing so much harm to our marriages. Let's learn more about each other's weaknesses and strengths; also, let us learn to tolerate each other so that together, we can build better and healthy nests for our families. In most homes, dads are seen as "lions" and moms as "angels" and so children are sometimes threatened that they would be reported to dad for doing something bad. By this, the kids grow associating their dads with *sternness* and wickedness. Eventually, fear replaces the love they have for their dad. The question is, what does this bring into the nest?

Preparing food for our spouses is another area the devil uses to raise confusion. For example, there has been times when I am busily preaching or in a religious meeting and I had to pause to answer a call from my husband. Mostly, he just wanted to confirm if the food at home was prepared by me. Severally, I had to suspend many programs to see to it that I have personally set the table for my husband or else I can be rest assured that, he was going to call me during

the program. Really? Yes! That's how sensitive the issue can become. It is worth noting that husbands enjoy what comes from their wives' pots than from other sources. Sometimes, it is clear that, he is at home and feeling lonely hence, he wants me to know that. The issue has got nothing to do with food.
He only needs my attention and so all things must wait for me to hear him.

This scenario can be the beginning of confusion in the home because, at any point, the devil is watching and waiting to raise tension and confusion. In our case, we made conscious efforts, though difficult, to prevent the devil from infiltrating our nest. Wives, no matter how busy you are, make time to serve the interest of your spouse and children, so they don't lack anything (Proverbs 31:10-11). This is a duty that we are responsible for, without any excuse whatsoever.

Finally, I must say that as women, we should remember to pray continuously and wait on the Lord to lead us. This is the surest way of preventing mistakes. For instance, in many cases we call our house helps many names which are not worth mentioning, and other times too, we entangle them in spells stories and many others. The point however is, if indeed you prayed and were led to have a particular person, what then would be the justification for all these? Will God mislead you in anyway? As we yearn to build the nest where peace and love reign, we must not fail in doing our duties (including praying).

Building requires much more than talking and taking personal decisions; God must lead for you to follow. Weaving a nest requires courage, strength, forgiveness, love and much patience.

Several factors such as in-laws' interference can make or break your marriage. Your marriage can be on the verge of breaking if your in-laws are bent on walking you out of your marital home. In fact, in some cases, in-laws can do everything spiritually, mentally, emotionally and physically possible to see you exit your marital home for reasons best known to them. In situations like this, you need to call on God the more and seek God's favour to really turn situations around. For example, after several years of Godless efforts to keep me from my home, kids and husband, my marriage still stood. In Matthew 19:6, God made it clear that if He joins together, no one can put asunder.

"So then, they are no longer two but one flesh. Therefore what God has joined together, let not man separate" (Matthew 19: 6).

God is and has been the pillar behind my marriage and so I believe that by His word, no one can break your marriage too. In my marriage life, I have always yearn to build a nest that is rooted and grounded in God for my family, therefore, during turbulent times, I kept my focus on God, and today, God is glorified. May any marriage that is going through turbulent times experience God's favour and be redeemed in Jesus' name.

CHARACTERISTICS
OF A
GOOD WOMAN

CHAPTER THREE

CHARACTERISTICS OF A GOOD WOMAN

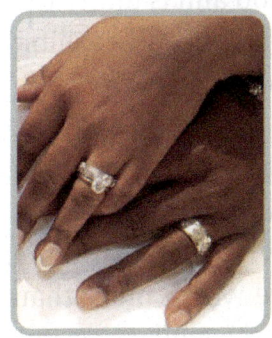

Proverbs 31:10-12

"Who can find a virtuous wife? For her worth is far above rubies. The heart of her husband safely trusts her; so he will have no lack of gain. She does him good and not evil. All the days of her life".

The word *"Virtuous"* can be translated as *"Excellent, Noble or Strong"*. It is used to describe God's strength. It depicts men who are self-motivated and heroic. In our context, it represents the strong character of the Proverbs 31 woman.

It applies to women who exhibit characteristics such as: loving, good, trustworthy, industrious, creative and skilled. A woman who is humble, discerning, organized, strong, dignified, compassionate and generous. She is unselfish, unworried, peaceful, confident, intelligent, productive, joyful, wise, disciplined, enterprising, responsible and authoritative.

A woman who seeks the face of God and is under the influence of the Spirit of God can practically exhibit these virtues. Clearly, these noble characters are available to all women who seek and believe in God. Nevertheless, women of these virtues are hard to come by and I must say not many can be found among millions of women. Women with these unique virtues are highly valued and are worth more than rubies. As mothers, we must train and raise our daughters to become one of the few women with these virtues and also hope and pray for our sons to meet and love women of this caliber.

Contemporarily, we place too much emphasis on outward appearance, pleasure, and entertainment which is not of interest to God.

I beseech you all to raise and teach your children in the Lord so that virtues such as the joy of productivity, discipline, accomplishment and hard work would be their way of life. A woman of this caliber's primary relationship is obviously rooted in her Lord. God has the first place in her life. Consequently, her other relationships are streamlined by God and in the right direction. This woman's husband has full confidence in her. And possibly, the two of them will live peacefully and share common goals and responsibilities for their family. The husband, as the Bible says, trusts his wife totally because, he knows that everything she does is for his own good and will promote the common good of the entire family.

The husband of this woman delegates responsibilities and authority to her without fear that she might take his place as head of the home. The woman is clear on her position as a woman and so will under no circumstance show disrespect or try to "lord" it over her husband. She will not unduly cease the opportunity given to her by her husband to disrespect him. Rather, this woman constantly has in mind that she complements and must be a true companion to her husband. What a fortunate husband! In fact, he has it all. The Bible confirms this position with God as it is written: a woman with good morals selects:

"Wool and flax and works with eager hands. She is like the merchant ships, bringing her food from afar. She gets up while it is still dark; she provides food for her family and portions for her servant girls. She considers a field and buys it out of her earnings she planted in a vineyard. She sets about her work vigorously; her arms are strong for her tasks. She sees that her trading is profitable, and her lamp does not go out at night. In her hand she holds the distaff and grasps the spindle with her fingers" (Proverbs 31:13-19)

Considering the scenarios above, I don't think it is wrong to say that such a woman is a wonderful home manager! This woman rises up early, which is a necessity to starting up a successful day. This woman is able to wake up in good time enough to seek the face of God and ask for further direction as to how to plan for the day's activities.

This woman is systematic in her way of doing things. She knows how to prepare delicious and healthy meals for her household.

She plans all her activities including menus, and the delegation of assignment to her servants. She is a business-minded woman who does genuine business that helps her to bring money home. She buys and sells wisely. She is trustworthy with money, handling the family accounts with sincerity. She engages in all kinds of business that would yield good money to support her family. She is extremely hardworking and delights in the fruits of her labour.

It really pays and it's refreshing to successfully accomplish a task in sincerity. The results are mostly positive and fulfilling. God in his own mercy made us ambitious and hence, appreciates hard work that produces good results to support His work and merry making.

"Then I commended mirths, because a man hath no better thing under the sun, than to eat, and to drink, and to be merry: For that shall abide with him of his labor the days of his life, which God giveth him under

the sun" (Ecclesiastes 8:15)
This woman is blessed with multi talents and she practically endeavours to take special interest in all she does and she also has knowledge in all aspects of the economy. The Bible is also clear on her involvement in farming. She and her husband raise sheep, and she carefully chooses the best wool, weaving it into garments. They raise flax and she weaves it into linen. She designs and sews clothes for herself, her children, and her servants. She also sells the products she makes for extra money.

Point is, this woman seems to be a perfect woman with no flaws at all and many women will feel that she is a super woman but, believe me, that is what happens when you seek God's face in all you do. Let all of us endeavour to emulate her examples.

HER
MODEST OUTWARD
APPEARANCE

CHAPTER FOUR

HER MODEST
OUTWARD APPEARANCE

Proverbs 3:20-27

"She opens her arms to the poor and extends her hands to the needy. When it snows, she has no fear for her household; for all of them are clothed in scarlet. She makes coverings for her bed; she is clothed in fine linen and purple.

Her husband is respected at the city gate, where he takes his seat among the elders of the land. She makes linen garments and sells them, and supplies the merchants with sashes. She is clothed with strength and dignity; she can laugh at the days to come.

30

She speaks with wisdom, and faithful instruction is on her tongue. She watches over the affairs of her household and does not eat the bread of idleness".

Considering all that this woman in Proverbs 31 does in a day, she is still able to keep herself attractive to meet her husband's sexual needs. She does not deny her husband sex neither does she give unreasonable excuses to her husband. By her deeds, her husband admires her and she also has influence over him. Her husband wins the admiration and respect of all the members in their community as a leader.

She is able to manage her home and so her husband has the time to be part and be much involved in community activities. She adequately prepares for events and she is always ready for the next activity or what must be done. I must be quick to add that her proactive nature is just spot on. Her family is properly clothed to meet the weather conditions at any point in time and she is kind enough to treat her maid servants well, as if they were her own family members. She actually provides for them as well and caters for them as she does for her own children.

Fascinatingly, the care of this woman we are learning from, for her family is not limited to material provision.

The Bible says *"she speaks with wisdom, and faithful instruction is on her tongue"*. True wisdom sources from God. Therefore by inference, we can confidently say that this woman knows God's word and she applies the word on a daily basis. I guess she extends her way of life beyond her immediate family to friends who need counsel and encouragement. She cares for the needy and she is compassionate and generous. In our time, charity homes have been institutionalized and so we overlook responsibilities and when we feel like aiding, we just give money and we are done. Though it's good, we need to be personally involved, because that's what the Bible says was done by the Proverbs 31 woman.

At the end of the day this woman is filled with much joy because, she knows that she has done everything she possibly can, to prepare her family for any eventuality, leaving the rest up to God. She trusts God unreservedly to supply whatever may become necessary to face unknown future possibilities; sickness, death, grief, loss or disability. This Godly woman fears the Lord indeed and she joyfully places the future in the hands of God. I believe that when we consider all that has been written about this woman, we will have no doubt about the reason why the Bible says:

"Her children arise and call her blessed; her husband also, and he praises her: Many women do noble things, but you surpass them all. Charm is deceptive and beauty is fleeting; but a woman who fears the Lord is to be praised. Give her the reward she has earned, and let her works bring her praise at the city gate"
(Proverbs 31:28-31).

As a writer and a woman of God, the Lord has enlightened me about this woman and I am burdened to share it with everyone so that, we can also use to the fullest our individual gifts from God. I am working hard to simply make the most of my own gift and I believe in a matter of time you will also make the full use of your talents and gifts.

The Power of Time:

The woman the Bible talks about in Proverbs 31 exhibited virtues that are worth emulating. Let me quickly say that, any woman who is focused and who understands her position as a woman can do the same or better if she constantly draws strength and direction from God. If we set our priorities right and back it with determination, I have no doubt that women of this present age and time can achieve a lot more. Considering the scope of the woman under consideration's deeds, one may think that she will not be able to do as much as she did, but the contemporary woman can equally achieve a lot if we have clear cut priorities and self-motivation.

The accounts in the Bible clearly project her strength which I think every woman of today should draw inspiration from and move ahead. We should be determined to accomplish more for the family and ourselves. As women, we should explore more and try hard to broaden our horizon in terms of managing our homes and pursuing our aspirations and dreams. All these should be geared towards building a healthy family.

A constant eye must be kept on distractions which are bound to come our way so that, in an event when the distractions are prevalent, we will not lose focus. Much concentration must be kept on our abilities, our aspirations and the available opportunities that will help in building and tending a Godly home.

You may think that the time spent in changing a house into a home is frustrating and imprisoning, but, believe me it's just a matter of time, the situation will change. Most women spend time in the home raising children and fixing all that needs to be done at home to keep the house intact. Sometimes however, it feels like they are not able to dress like other ladies; they are not able to go to places like other women are doing and many compare themselves with others, whether positive or negative.

Listen, there are times and seasons for doing things, as the Bible says. It is for this reason that as women, we must make time to advance our career as we manage the home, because, eventually, the situation will change and we will be idle. At that time, it might be too late for you to advance your career.

The woman in Proverbs 31 proved herself strong, hence, she was able to achieve more to meet the standard at any point in time. This is what we need as women today, so that we are constantly able to do more to keep our marriages, our children as well as our career.

Building the home is also a career which requires much energy and time. Our mentor (the Proverbs 31 woman) built her home with all that she had. She discharged her duties gladly, fearlessly and creatively without murmuring and complaining. It is clear that this woman's first and foremost priority was positively building her home. As time went on, she also ensured that she developed her interest and increased her line of duties so that as her children grew up and required less attention or went to school, she could have much more doing to keep her from lazing around.

This is what I am talking about. This is what a woman of today should embrace. Mothers, we have no excuse at all! Let's rise up and take position so that we can grow spiritually, emotionally, intellectually, materially and in all the aspects that we can think about to help support the family. Readers, let's encourage ourselves and our younger generation of women to continue to develop themselves even if all their time is being consumed by raising their kids. Situations change over time and every woman must aspire to have the best of the situation. Once upon a time, you were a girl, then you became a wife and eventually a mother. Each and every stage requires different skills and strength.

Thus, as a woman, never give up your motherhood or womanhood responsibilities, and don't also burry your special interests because of a current situation which cannot be permanent. Any woman who stops sharpening her skills due to raising kids is making an unpardonable mistake, because when these kids leave the nest, what will you be doing then? As a young mother, continue developing yourself spiritually, academically and socially so that you can face challenges at any time of your life.

SETTING
PROPER
PRIORITIES

CHAPTER FIVE

SETTING PROPER PRIORITIES

Proverbs 31: 27
"She watches over the affairs of her household and does not eat the bread of idleness".

Setting priorities is a skill that must not be overlooked as women. As a woman, you must set your priority list to guide your path. God must come first on the list, whether you are married or not. Most married women have high expectations of their husbands to provide all their needs, relegating God to the background.

This eventually turns husbands in to their "God" which is against the almighty God's intention. God is a jealous God and will not allow any human being to take His place. Your spouse should follow God on the list, children, if any, come next and others follow, based on God's leading and direction. Having a priority list keeps you focused at every point in time and it also ensures that you use resources judiciously to the benefit of all.

The Position of Children in Building the Nest:
Raising up children is so demanding and draining. It is very easy to unconsciously consider your husband after dealing with your children. This certainly alters the position of husbands on the priority scale. One day during a usual chat between my husband and myself, I asked him about how he felt about our union, and quickly he referred to when we first got married. Implying that, it was only the two of us. But now, kids and other duties have taken my attention too.

In fact, I sensed jealousy and I must say that, as a woman, you need to carefully plan your duties so that each member of the family get the attention he or she deserves. This also brought to mind the little frictions and arguments we had as I ignored him and attended to our little kid. I did not understand it at the time, but, I think Paul, my husband, felt the shift in his position on the priority scale and I think he also felt he was gradually losing the attention I used to give him. Following the priority scale and giving everyone the attention they deserve can be very stressful but, truly, each and every one of them must be catered for. The needs of the children must be taken care of, without making the husband feel that his place has been taken by the kids or else he will certainly see them as intruders! The issue is a very sensitive one but, as women, we are up to the task.

For every woman, God, husband and children should lead the priority table and then, you can reach out to others. Interestingly, you the woman come last. If we inter change any of these positions, we will get ourselves into trouble. Again, if we put other people before our families, we will regret it. And if we put ourselves ahead of everybody else, we are certainly going to regret it.

The Fruit of Singleness.

As a single person, you certainly will have a different set of priorities and I also think that at this stage in your life as a woman, you have every opportunity to serve God with sincerity of heart. Serving God wholeheartedly must be your first desire, your education, getting a rewarding job and thinking of how best you can support and influence other people's lives, must be your order of priorities. You may not at this stage have children, all things being equal, unless you are helping raise children that are not biologically yours. As a single person, you are free from all the challenges that distract couples, hence, you are at liberty to develop a very good relationship with God and reach out to many other people.

You have the opportunity of participating in all church activities and influencing a large group of people at school, place of work, neighbourhood and many other areas of your jurisdiction. It is important to live above reproach, as a single person, so that you can have a greater sphere of influence. Excellence, integrity and purity of heart must be virtues that you possess or aspire to have.

Do not be blown away by any wind or live your life anyhow but rather, see yourself to have much to offer in this world. At this stage you have every given opportunity to use your gift and talent from God to impact and influence all the people that you have encounters with.

My dear reader, whether married or single, do not be buried in seeking to satisfy your personal need and wants alone. Reach out to as many people as possible to ensure that you cease all available opportunities. I therefore challenge you to look at your priorities again and ensure that the scale is in place. Our way of life and our ability to lead others to serve God for eternal life is all that matters in life.

Scripture says that:
"He hath made everything beautiful in his time: also he hath set the world in their hearts, so that no man can find out the work that God maketh from the beginning to the end" (Eccle.3:11).

Judgment and eternal life are real. Our God has placed eternity in our hearts. I must say that every one of us craves for greater accomplishments that might not even contribute to eternal life. As a Godly married woman, building a Godly home is an achievement that cannot be overemphasized and it is actually expected of every good woman. Building a Godly home is a priority that can be achieved through God's leading and drawing strength from God as well. I hope and pray that all those I am reaching through this book will not just read and take the words for granted and will also not be as Ezekiel's thoughtless and hypocritical listeners in the Bible.

"But, the house of Israel will not hearken unto thee; for they will not hearken unto me: for all the house of Israel are impudent and are hard-hearted. Behold, I have made thy face strong against their faces and thy forehead strong against their foreheads"
(Ezekiel 3:7-8).

Finally, my fellow women, I desire that, as you read these words, you will pay heed to God's words in obedience and really put into practice these words of encouragement so that our way of life and our marriages will bring glory to God.

6

PRAYER
LINES

CHAPTER SIX

PRAYER LINES

I Thessalonians 5:16 -18
"Rejoice evermore. Pray without ceasing. In everything give thanks: for this is the will of God in Christ Jesus concerning you"

As two different beings raised separately come together as a couple, there are bound to be frictions and hitches in terms of petty or major quarrels or fights. Whether you are just starting to fight tooth and nail to save it like I did, please get it, read it, live by it to help you live in love with your soul mate.

I used to pray for a blue print, steps, or a road map on how as a wife, I could make my husband happy so we could become soul mates to raise a Godly family. Take my word for it; it is only God that has the miracle of making your marriage the best it can be. I wish I knew this years ago; I believe the situation would have been different. Words are powerful and can cut deep in the heart. For example; "I love you, but, I am not in love with you." These words really cut to the core of my heart because, these are powerful words.

Today, there are several marriages that are struggling and are on the rocks but, believe me, there are many ways of rescuing and saving the situation no matter the shape. In my case, it was my passion to save my marriage and I hope and pray that, it will be your desire too, if your marriage is struggling. I strongly believed in God and believed in my family, hence, took stock of my ways and changed my strategy more towards God until my husband and I became one again.

The condition of my family and how happy we are is all that matters to me. This is my choice and passion and will hold on to it until God calls me to glory.

The prayers I said at the time reversed and saved the situation and I want to use this opportunity to share them with you. I hope and pray that you will back it with faith so that these prayers will be your source of strength and further bring salvation to your marriage.

David's Prayer (1 Chronicles 29:10-19):

Praise be to you, God of our fathers. From everlasting to everlasting you are LORD; your greatness and your power and your glory and your majesty and your splendour, for everything in heaven and earth is yours. You are exalted as head over everything. Wealth and honour come from you; you are the ruler of all things. In your hands are strength and power to exalt and give strength to all. Now, my God, I give you thanks and praise in your mighty name. "But who am I, and who are my people, that you are so generous to?

Everything comes from you, and we have given you only what comes from your hand. We are foreigners and strangers in your sight, just as my ancestors. Our days on earth are like a shadow, without hope.

LORD our God, all this abundance that we provided for building your temple for your Holy Name comes from your hand, and all of it belongs to you. I know, my God, that you test the heart and are pleased with integrity.

All these things I have given willingly and with honest intent. And now I have seen how willingly your people who are here have given to you. The God of our fathers Abraham, Isaac and Israel, keep these desires and thoughts in the hearts of your servant forever, and keep my heart loyal to you. And give your servant the wholehearted devotion to keep your command in the name of Jesus, AMEN!

Prayer for Couples:

Lord, help us remember when we first met and the strong love that grew between us. Help us to work this love into practical things so that nothing divides us. We ask for words that are kind and loving for each other. We also ask that our hearts always be ready to forgive each other as well as other people as you do. God, forgive us our trespasses. In Jesus name, AMEN!

Prayer of Confession:

Hallelujah, father, I confess my sins to you, that I am a sinner with unclean lips but, your word says if I confess my sins to you, you are faithful and just to forgive me. Father LORD, bless me and keep me; make your face shine upon me and be gracious to me; LORD turn your face towards me and give me peace (Numbers 6: 24-26). I am the seed of Abraham through Christ Jesus and I receive the blessing of Abraham. My sins are forgiven and I am blessed (Rom 4-7). Lord, bless my end more than my beginning (Job 42:12). Thank you Lord. I know you will favour me because, my enemies do not triumph over me (Psalm 41:11). I cover myself, my husband, my family, my children, my friends, my neighbours and my possessions with the blood of Jesus. Let the fire of God surround me and protect my life from destruction, my children from destruction, my husband from destruction and my family from destruction. Let angels from you my Lord, encamp around me and protect my children, my husband and my family (Psalm 34:7).The name of Jesus is my strong tower; I run into it and I am safe. (Proverbs 18:10) In the shadow of your wings will I trust. AMEN!

Marriage Restoration Prayer:

This is a powerful prayer for marriage restoration, I pray it will inspire, motivate and encourage you:

Lord God, Maker of miracles, I give you glory, honour and praise. Lord, I lift up my marriage to you. I pray that my heart will be filled with love and tenderness towards my spouse. I pray that you minister to my emotions so that my emotions become harmonious with your plans and purposes. May I receive your strength and your supernatural ability to reach out and show amazing love to my mate. I declare that I will continually draw near to you, and I will be open to your biblical words. I declare that I will allow you to guide me towards your will and your way.

By faith I believe that our marriage will become more and more pleasing in your eyes. Blessed be the Lord God of the universe who has supernatural joy, harmony, and peace for those who yield unto Him. In Jesus' name I pray, Amen. !

Wives, please adopt this prayer and believe in it and it will work for you and your marriage.

Prayer to change your attitude towards your husband:

I pray for my husband, the head of my household and priest of my home, I plead the blood of Jesus on his behalf and I ask that you God will heal me as a wife so that I no longer say or do anything that could inflict pain on my husband. I ask that you perfect my thoughts, my attitude, and my words towards my husband so that, I will no longer hurt him. May my thoughts be your thoughts and my words be your words. By your power, your goodness, and your mercy, I declare that I will have more healing in the area of having good attitude towards my husband. In the name of Jesus Christ, I bind all satanic forces that will try to come against me in achieving my objective as a good wife. I declare that I am being moulded to be a great wife and a mighty servant of God. AMEN!

Prayer for Children (Ephesians 3: 17-19):

My children are rooted and established in love. I pray that they may have power with all the saints to grasp in width, length, breadth and depth the love of Christ towards them. I pray that these children will experience this love that surpasses knowledge and that they may be filled to the measure of the fullness of God. In Ephesians 5:1 and 2:1, your word says my children will be imitators of God and live a life of love. They will submit to others out of reverence to Christ. I believe in your words Lord and I further pray that as your word says in Ephesians 6:1&2; my children will obey their parents in the Lord. They will honour their father and mother so that it may go well with them and that they may enjoy long life on earth. Amen!

In 1 Timothy 4:12, God has declared that no one will look down on my children, because I stand in the gap to plead the blood of Jesus to protect and guide them from the hand of the wicked. I bind the power of the enemy around them and I plead to ensure that the enemy does not have any legal foothold to attack them. Thank you Lord that my children will not forget your benefits. I pray that you forgive all their sins and heal all their diseases. I also pray that you salvage their lives from the pit, and crown them with love and compassion. I once again pray that you satisfy their souls with good things so that their youth is renewed like the eagle. My children will not walk in the counsel of the ungodly or stand in the path of sinners or sit in the seat of scoffers.

But, their delight will be in the law of you Lord and on your law they will meditate day and night. They will be like trees planted by the rivers of water which yield their fruit in season and whose leaves will not whither. My children will prosper in whatever they do. AMEN!

GODLY DECLARATIONS:
- *I come this day to put on the **Belt** of **Truth**.*
- *I acknowledge that I need truth. I need to be dedicated to truth. I need to follow the truth of your Word.*
- *Lord, I need to make reading your Word a priority in my life. If I sincerely open my mind to your Word, then I will see the truth about what I need to increase in my life and what I need to decrease in my life.*
- *As I am praying this prayer, I realize that the enemy of my soul wants to condemn me for my failures.*
- *I declare that I will not let the enemy condemn me for my lack of success, because you are pleased with me when I try. You want me to learn to be content in doing my best. You want me to love myself anyway, just as you do.*

- *I put on the **Breastplate of Righteousness**.*
- *I acknowledge that I am able to wear this **Breastplate** because Jesus took my sins and gave me His righteousness.*
- *Lord, I will remind myself today of the enormous price Jesus paid so that I could be set free. Jesus did not take sin lightly, and I will not take sin lightly too.*
- *I will show my respect for you Lord, by seeking to obey you and seeking to please you this day.*
- *I put on the **Shoes** of **Peace**.*
- *I thank you for the peace I have about my future home in heaven. I feel restful and serene when I think about the glorious place where I will spend eternity.*
- *Jesus told us that He will give us peace. Father God, I want to feel peaceful in my daily life. I want to feel calm and content as I move through my day.*
- *By the power of Jesus Christ, I declare that today I will grow in my ability to live in peace.*
- *I will reject worry and fear. I will remember to trust you through all the circumstances of my day. I will not be moved by what I see or hear.*

- *I will be moved by what the Bible says. Your promises are true. Your promises are backed by the honour of your name.*
- *I put on the **Helmet** of **Salvation**. I thank you for my eternal salvation, and I thank you for the saving power of Jesus Christ that works daily in my life - helping me to defeat sin and helping me to put on the love of Christ.*

Thank you that you are renewing my mind and showing me how to defeat my wrong thoughts and wrong attitudes. Thank you that you are taking me from the way I have always been to the Godly way I can be through the power of Jesus Christ.

Binding and Breaking the Devil

I will feed my faith today. My faith will grow stronger this day. I will meditate on your promises to take care of me. When the enemy sends fiery darts my way - in order to discourage me or get me to doubt you - I will raise my shield of faith and deflect his attacks. My shield is a shield of confidence that you, God, are able to take care of me. I will continually remind myself of your faithfulness. In the name of Jesus Christ, my Lord and Saviour, I bind all principalities, powers of the air, wickedness in high places, thrones, dominions, world rulers and strong men exerting influence over my life, my workplace and my finances; I forbid they operate against me and against my family. In the name of Jesus, I bind and break witchcraft, mind-binding spirits, , destruction, lust, perversion, intimidation, rebellion, rejection, Schizophrenia, paranoia, anger, hatred, wrath and rage, resentment, bitterness, unforgiveness, slander, deception, doubt and unbelief, passivity, pride, false humility and spirits that block mind control. In the name of Jesus, I bind and break the spirits of Ahab and Jezebel, fear, hypnosis and hypnotic trance, rock music, greed, addiction, drugs, alcohol and compulsive behaviour. In the name of Jesus, I bind kings, princes, and world rulers for each spirit named.

I strip each spirit and his hierarchy off their power, armour and rank, and separate each from the other. I speak confusion to the ranks of the enemy, and declare their assignments against me are hereby rendered null and void. In the name of Jesus, I bind and break all evil affecting my sense of sight, smell, taste, touch, hearing, my emotions and all evil plans against the seven points of my body used by witchcraft – the base of the spine, spleen, navel, heart, throat, between the eyes, and the top of the head. In the name of Jesus, I bind and break *all evil spirits in my reproductive, skeletal, muscular, digestive, excretory, endocrine, respiratory, circulatory, and nervous systems. In the name of Jesus, I bind and break any and all evil powers giving aid or pulling these systems in my body toward evil; by means of energy drawn from the sun, moon, stars, planets, constellations, earth, air, wind, fire, water, light, darkness, matter, elements or from lines, squares, circles, symbols, artefacts and/or potions against us.*

In the name of Jesus, I bind and break any transference of spirits from family, friends or associates of people for whom I pray. I forbid transfer of spirits – those that will curse me. With the sword of the Holy Spirit and the blood of Jesus, I cover my mind, emotions and will, preventing soul ties from ever being re-established. I declare these in the name of Jesus.

I pray for all as well as the person uttering this prayer in the name of Jesus, spirits from the netherworld, spirits between, over and around those praying and those listening, and all familiar spirits are completely bound and forbidden to manifest in the name of Jesus. In the name of Jesus, I bind and break the power of all curses spoken, all rituals or sacrifices, all divination, *spells, incantations, meditations, and all sorcery or magic. In the name of Jesus, I place a shield of **Faith** over the minds of all to protect them against infiltration from end-time mind control.*

Thank you Father, that no weapon formed against me shall prosper, because I am covered by the blood of Jesus, and You God have put all things under your feet (Isaiah 54:17, Ephesians 1:22); Because Christ dwells in me, I declare that greater is He that is in me than he that is in the world. Lord, I will be unwavering in my devotion to you this day.

The Sword of the Spirit which is the Word of God
Speaking based on scripture, Lord, I remind myself that when I speak your scripture, your power is unleashed. You have given believers words that will change the world. Lord, I dedicate my mouth to you. I want all my words to please you. Help me gain greater control over my tongue. I declare that today I will use my tongue to bless others, and I will avoid strife and unnecessary conflict. Father, as I live this time of prayer, I am going to be a freshly focused follower of Jesus Christ! Halleluiah

Prayer for the Sick

Heavenly Father, You are my Creator, and you are my Healer. You are Jehovah Rapha - the God who heals. You have compassion for us in our sicknesses and our pain. Your mercy is from everlasting to everlasting. I come to you this day, asking you to heal my body. I ask you to go into each cell and correct whatever is wrong. Father, bring healing, harmony, and unity to every cell, every organ, and every system in my body. I ask that you heal the root of any pain that I experience. Thank you that you are repairing everything that has to do with my body. Right now I am giving you my fears and my worries. I pick up the shield of faith and draw confidence that you are working on my behalf this day, Amen.

Dear Lord, I come to you not satisfied with staying average, not satisfied with just the traditional, not satisfied with the way it has always been. I press unto you that I may come up higher. I am open to you. I want to experience your new things in your perfect timing. I pick up confidence that I will hear clearly your voice and understand how to follow you. I pick up confidence that you are going to lead me away from sickness and

weakness and lead me towards health and healing.
AMEN!

Prayer for the Nation
Oh God in heaven, I come before you in the name of Jesus on behalf of the leaders of (name the nation). First of all in accordance with your word (I Timothy 2:1-2), I intercede and give thanks for kings and all in authority, that, we all will live a quiet and peaceful life.

I pray for the word of God to deliver us all from unreasonable and wicked leaders (II Thessalonians 3:1-2). The heart of the king is in your hand and you can turn it which ever way you choose (Proverbs 21:1). I ask that you direct the heart and mind of our leaders to make decisions that will lead the country in your way and according to your word. I thank you Lord, for bringing change to the politics of our nation. Thank you for changing the voices of influence to speak in agreement with your Word. I ask that you send labourers filled with the spirit of wisdom and might, to surround our leaders and provide them with Godly counsel and insight.

I also ask that, you remove from positions of authority those who stubbornly oppose righteousness and replace them with men and women who follow You Lord and Your appointed course. As we enter the final hours of these last days, I ask for the spirit of faith, the workings of miracles for signs, wonders, gifts and demonstrations of the Holy Spirit and power to be in strong operation. Let believers in our nation and on every land be unified to stand strong by faith in Jesus, the anointed One and His anointing, that His glory may be revealed all over the earth.

Prayer of Thanksgiving

Thank you father in the name of Jesus. I give you glory and honour. You are holy, you are mighty, you are good, you are loving and you are kind. You are the God of the universe, all powerful, all knowing, all sufficient, ancient of days, the I am that I am, worthy is the Lamp that was slain to receive power and riches, wisdom, strength, honour, glory and blessing in Jesus name. AMEN!

CONCLUSION

"Mothers Nest", is a blessing to me and I just wish I had this knowledge earlier in my marriage life. However, I thank God that I have it now. As believers, we know that God works everything together for our good and in his own time He provides us with what we really need. The information in this book is so powerful for any marriage and I believe that this book will bring much knowledge to all who read it. I also hope and trust that God will use this book to save many marriages.

The Proverbs 31 woman that this book drew inspiration from was not a doormat. She was not miserable, waiting to get out of the house to "find herself." In fact, she was the queen of her home and family. And there was a wide range of opportunities opened to her which she did not let go unutilized. Seriously, there was no area of her culture that she did not influence. She had enough energy to get involved with, or supervise virtually everything that mattered to her and her family. She participated in education, charity, business, manufacturing, sales, land investment, agriculture, ranching, you name it.

This virtuous woman as the Bible describes her is worth knowing about. In the last chapter of this book, different kinds of prayers have been offered. I must say that these are prayers that I have no doubt at all concerning the miraculous results that would come up if believed and said in sincerity. I used these prayers daily to save my marriage and hope they help you save or improve your marriage too.

At the time, I searched long and hard to get materials of this kind, but could not find any. But, at God's own appointed time He, God sent it to me. My intention is not just to convince you as a reader or just to write for the world to know that I can write. Instead, I present this book as a tool from God, through me, to straighten every crooked, bitter, sour, tattered and unfruitful marriage.

This book is also meant to provide direction and guidance to young ladies who are not yet married, so that, eventually when they marry, they can have a good marriage and raise Godly homes. May the blessings that I have received from this wisdom find you in Jesus's name.

Lightning Source UK Ltd.
Milton Keynes UK
UKOW07f2334270217
295497UK00010B/54/P